GIVEN TO _Bernard_

FROM _The Satterwhite_

DATE _July 18 - 1974_

Pebbles in the sand give a foundation on which to stand.

Pebbles In The Sand

By Donald E. Wildmon

★ ★ ★ ★ ★
Five Star Publishers
Box 1368
Tupelo, Mississippi 38801

SET UP, PRINTED, AND BOUND BY THE
PARTHENON   PRESS,   AT   NASHVILLE,
TENNESSEE, UNITED STATES OF AMERICA

FOR
BILL AND ELOISE
The parents of my wife—

Other Books By Donald E. Wildmon

LEAVES OF SILVER
THOUGHTS WORTH THINKING
A GIFT FOR LIVING
TREASURED THOUGHTS
STEPPING STONES
NUGGETS OF GOLD
PRACTICAL HELP FOR DAILY LIVING

More than 100,000 copies of Donald E. Wildmon's books now in print.

Ask for them at your bookstore.

Five Star Publishers
Box 1368
Tupelo, Mississippi 38801

"Good Reading Comes From Five Star"

ABOUT THE AUTHOR

A United Methodist minister who seeks to extend his ministry beyond the pulpit, Donald E. Wildmon has found wide acceptance to his writing. In addition to his books, he is the author of a weekly inspirational column which appears in many newspapers and magazines across the country.

Mr. Wildmon is minister of the Lee Acres United Methodist Church in Tupelo, Mississippi. A person who loves to travel, he annually leads a tour of the Holy Land. Christians from around the nation join him on these tours. He extends an invitation to any who would like to go on one of his tours to contact him through the publishers.

Mr. Wildmon is a native of Ripley, Mississippi. He graduated from Millsaps College with a BA and earned his BD from Emory University.

THE PEBBLES

A Pebble On:
CROSSING RIVERS

Matthew 6:34—"Therefore do not be anxious about tomorrow, for tomorrow will be anxious for itself. Let the day's own trouble be sufficient for the day."

Abraham Lincoln and some of his friends were once forced to do some traveling during a very rainy season. They had crossed many small streams and the water was high and fast in all of them. After a long day of facing streams that nearly washed them away, they came to a lodge where they spent the night.

Sitting around the fire that night, the men were talking about how high the streams were and how fast the water was flowing. Then someone brought up the fact that the very next day the group would be forced to cross Fox River. Fox River was very difficult to cross even when the water was low, and if it was up in comparison to the other streams it would be nearly impossible to cross.

As they sat around and talked, many expressed the thought that Fox River would be uncrossable. Since they had a date to keep, it was important to the traveling group that they not be delayed on their journey.

For some time that night the group sat around discussing the river, and the awful possibilities that would be opened to them when it came time to cross it. Following some discussion of the river, someone noticed

11

that there was a Methodist preacher spending the night in the lodge who traveled the territory quite often and was very familiar with Fox River. One of the group asked the preacher about Fox River and how he managed to cope with it when the water was high. "Preacher, you have been listening to us talk about Fox River. Do you have any special way of getting across that river, any rules to follow that might help us?" a member of the group asked.

"Well, now that you asked," replied the preacher, "I do have one fixed rule about that river. I've crossed it many times and I know it is a mighty problem to get across sometimes. But I have solved the problem with just one rule." "What's your secret, preacher? Have you got a special place to cross?" they asked.

"Nope, haven't got a special place to cross. I always cross it where everyone else does," he said. "Then you must have a float put back nearby to help you cross it," one of the group stated.

"Nope, haven't got a float put back. Just never did have the time to build one for the occasion, and didn't have the money to buy one," said the preacher. "But you said you had a rule about crossing that river!" one of the Lincoln group blurted out. "If you haven't got a special place to cross, or a float to cross on, then tell us what your rule about crossing the river is!"

"Well, sir," said the preacher, "I've crossed Fox River many times. But I have learned never to cross it till I reach it." And with that the preacher rolled over and went to sleep.

You know, it's a pretty good rule to follow.

A Pebble On:
WHAT DO YOU SAY WHEN YOU DIE?

Proverbs 29:23—"A man's pride will bring him low, but he who is lowly in spirit will obtain honor."

His name was Thomas Jefferson. He was born at Shadwell, Virginia, on April 13, 1743. He died on July 4, 1826. The date was a tribute to the man. And in between those two dates he tied together a life of service to his fellowman.

You probably remember him as the author of the Declaration of Independence. And most of all, he would have wanted you to remember him for that. He even wrote his own epitaph. He had a reason for doing so. Before his death, he gave his daughter Martha Randolph instructions to have these words inscribed on his headstone: "Here was buried Thomas Jefferson, author of the Declaration of American Independence, of the Statute of Virginia for Religious Freedom, and father of the University of Virginia."

That is saying a lot about a man's life—any man's life. Jefferson could have put more on that headstone, you know. He could have added a long list of accomplishments. He could have stated that he had served the state of Virginia as its governor. Most of us, had we the honor of being governor, would have included it in our epitaph. For we would have wanted others to know. But not Jefferson. Also, he could have stated that he was a member of Congress. For he was. But he did not choose to include that fact on his headstone.

Jefferson could also have reminded those who were to view his headstone of the fact that he was minister to France. And Secretary of State. He was that, you recall, under the administration of George Washington. And that would have been something worth recalling for most of us. But not for Jefferson.

From that position Jefferson moved up to the number two man of these United States. He served as Vice-President under John Adams. But not even that was included on his headstone.

Or, had he wished, Jefferson could have had engraved on his headstone the fact that he was President of this country. Not once, but twice! And that is an honor shared by very, very few men. But Jefferson did not consider even that fact worthy to be included in his most precious accomplishments.

Most of us would agree that pride is often a vice that destroys many of us. We accomplish something and we cannot wait for the world to learn of our deed and praise us for doing it. And many of us keep telling people years after our accomplishment of what we once did.

Some people learn how to handle pride. Jefferson was such a man. He learned how like all people do who do so—through a great desire to be a servant. Why didn't Jefferson include all those other accomplishments on his headstone? He told his daughter when she sought

14

the reason: "The things that are not on my inscription are the things the people did for me," he said. "The things that are on it are things I did for the people."

That's proper control of pride. Pray to God that we can all acquire it.

A Pebble On:
THEIR SON CAME HOME

I Corinthians 13:4a—"Love is patient and kind . . ."

I ran across a story in my reading once which I wish to pass along to you. I think it has something of a moral in it.

Back during the Second World War the parents of a sailor went for several weeks without hearing anything from their son. Finally, they gave up on their son and considered him a war victim. However, near the end of the war the parents, who lived in New Jersey, received a phone call from someone in San Diego, California. After a moment on the phone, the parents recognized the voice as that of their son. He was alive!

During the course of the conversation the son explained to his parents that for the past several months he had found it difficult to write because he had been taking care of a war victim. He told them that the person had been wounded in the war and had lost a leg, an arm, an eye, and part of his face.

His parents expressed concern over the poor sailor and then bragged on their son for taking care of him during all those months. The boy then asked his parents for permission to bring the boy home to live with them. He explained that the boy didn't have another home nor anyone to care for him. His parents expressed their concern for the wounded sailor and also told their son that they thought it was very noble of him to want to bring the sailor home with him. But after some conversation, the parents expressed their desire to their son that he not bring the boy home with him. They simply didn't want the job of taking care of such a battle-scarred sailor. Their son said he understood their feelings and said that he would not bring the boy home. Expressing his love for the parents, the sailor son hung up.

You know, I guess it is hard to fulfill such a request as the sailor son made. For most of us don't want a disfigured person around the house, do we? None of us like to look at ugly things, and most of us judge a person's beauty by their physical appearance. We appreciate the good that those who are disfigured have done. But we would just rather not have to be burdened with them around the house.

Many times we feel sorry for the physically handicapped. So we give some little something that requires no effort on our part and does them little good. But I think what the handicapped person wants more than anything else is to be treated like a human being.

The morning after they spoke with their son, the couple in New Jersey received a telegram from the Naval officials stating that their son had jumped from a window to his death. The parents couldn't understand why their son had reacted so to their request until the body arrived and the casket was opened. Their son had only one arm, one leg, one eye, and a badly disfigured face.

Maybe we should try a little harder to love those who want to be treated like a human being.

A Pebble On:
PROGRESS! ISN'T IT A WONDERFUL THING!

Proverbs 14:12—"There is a way which seems right to a man, but its end is the way of death."

Progress! Isn't it a wonderful thing!

For instance, abortion was once illegal except for exceptional cases. But now—now we have progressed! In more and more of our states abortion—for any reason at all—is not only legal but encouraged! An abortion on an embryo of eight months is quite legal and accepted now, and most expecting mothers who do so have an abortion simply because they don't want the child! Maybe in the future if the mother decides shortly after the boby is born that she doesn't want it—the wrong sex, deformed, wrong color hair, ears too red—she can simply send it to an incinerator to be burned. And if you think that progress isn't getting closer, just give us time. Closer and closer we are coming to Hitler's master race. We are building what we fought to destroy. Progress! Isn't it a wonderful thing!

Or, again, see the progress in another area—freedom of expression. Our progress has legalized pornography on the newsstand and in the movie while outlawing prayer and Bible reading in public schools! Isn't progress simply wonderful!

See it still on another front—this wonderful thing we call progress. It has made the criminal socially respectable and the Christian socially rejectable. We coddle the criminal and condemn the Christian. Progress! Isn't it simply wonderful!

Then there is scientific progress. Man splits the atom! And the first thing he does with his new knowledge is to make a bomb to kill his fellowman. Progress! It is so fantastic it is killing us!

We used to judge the rightness or the wrongness of a deed by a Higher Power. Now we put it up to popular vote—"everybody does it." Progress is simply great!

We build sprawling cities of architectural beauty— magnificent things! But we do not bother to learn our neighbor's name. Isn't progress simply grand!

We used to rest one day in seven—most of us. A few who absolutely had to worked. Now that seventh day can hardly be distinguished from the other six. More and more businesses are opening to "serve" the people. What we did call greed is now called service. Oh, this thing called progress is simply the most!

There is still other evidence of our progress. We feel sorry for the dope addict. We protect him, defend him, provide him with some juice for his habit. And we chastize the total adstainer for being non-social. Progress! How do we manage to get so much of it!

We raise our prices so we can cut them when we put our products on sale. We run the speedometer mileage indicator back to sell the car. What we once called unethical business practices are now good business procedures. Isn't progress truly wonderful!

In the Church folks used to have to give evidence that they should be admitted. Now the Church officials won't let them out. Progress! How great it is!

Progress is getting to be so great and grand that one wonders how long we will be able to stand it.

A Pebble On:
IF YOU CAN'T SING, WHITTLE!

I Corinthians 12:4—"To each is given the manifestation of the Spirit for the common good."

He was a lad in the town of Cremona, Italy, in the middle of the 17th century. Cremona was a musical town and great acclaim was given to those who could sing or play. Wanting to be accepted and given some recognition for his musical talents, he tried singing. His friends called him "squeaky voice" and he soon realized that his singing would never be anything special.

The young lad then tried to learn to play, but his success wasn't much better than his singing. So he was a dejected lad as he walked through the streets of Cremona with his friends and listened to their beautiful voices. About the only thing the lad could do was to whittle on a block of wood with his knife.

One day he was sitting on the edge of the street whittling as three of his friends played and sang beautiful songs for the people passing by. Appreciating the musical ability of his friends, many people dropped some coins into their hands to reward their efforts. One gentlemen stopped longer than many of the others and even asked the friends to sing a song again. After they finished he dropped a coin into the hand of the singer.

Then he moved on down the street.

Upon looking, the boys discovered that it was a gold coin! It was quite a piece of money to give a street singer. But the man who gave it could afford to do so. "Who was he?" asked the lad who whittled. "It was Amati," his friend with the beautiful voice replied. "Amati who?" asked the lad. "Nicolo Amati," the friend replied. "He is the greatest violin maker in all of Italy!"

That evening at home the lad thought about the man named Nicolo Amati. He was a man who succeeded in the musical field. But he neither sang nor played! The more he thought about the violin maker, the more he became convinced that he wanted to become a violin maker. He wanted to become the best violin maker in Italy!

Early the next morning the lad hurried off to the home of Nicolo Amati. Inquiring about the way, he sat on the doorsteps after arriving and waited for the great violin maker to come out. When Amati came out, the lad told him that he wanted to become a violin maker and asked Amati if he would teach him to make violins. He explained to Amati that he couldn't sing or play, but that he could whittle. And, more than anything else, he wanted to make violins.

Amati accepted the young lad as a pupil. Day after day, week after week, month after month, year after year the young man studied from the master. In due time his work became known in Cremona, then Italy, and finally throughout the whole world.

We may not have the talent to do some things as well as other people. But God has given us all a very special talent which, if we develop, can help us help others. Antonio Stradivari found this to be true. Even to this very day men still make music with his violins. And they pay upwards of $100,000 to do so!

Just because you can't sing or play doesn't mean you can't make music.

A Pebble On:
PRACTICING THE GOLDEN RULE

Luke 6:31—"And as you wish that men would do to you, do so to them."

Anthony Pino, age 9, came running into his home one afternoon shouting to his mother that his three older brothers had fallen into a pond and needed help. It happened when one of the brothers, Ruben, jumped on a plank floating in the pond north of Walsenburg, Colorado, and paddled away from the shore. He lost balance and fell into the pond. Ruben, 12, called for help. Two other brothers—Freddie, 13, and Richard, 10—both went into the pond to save Ruben.

Since none of the boys could swim, Anthony ran home to get help. Mrs. Fred Pino picked up the phone to call for help. Two people were talking on the party line. Mrs. Pino explained the situation to them and asked them to please hang up so she could call for help for her boys. The other two people refused to hang up. They laughed and ridiculed Mrs. Pino. She begged them to please get off the line, that her boys were drowning. They refused to do so, continued to laugh and ridicule.

Another lady in the home with Mrs. Pino took the receiver, spoke to the other two people, told them again what had happened, and asked them to please let Mrs. Pino use the phone to call for help. She, too, was met with a similar answer.

Reading such a story, one wonders how any two people could be so cruel and heartless. A mother, pleading for only the use of a phone for a few minutes in order to call for help for her drowning sons, was laughed at, ridiculed, refused.

The story isn't new. As much as we talk about the goodness of man, there remains always the evilness and sinfulness of man. Our Heavenly Father knows something about this type of sinfulness. While He was pleading and begging people to listen, they were intent on carrying His Son to the crucifixion site. While He attempted to be heard, they laughed and ridiculed Him.

Just common courtesy would have dictated that one should share a party line with one's neighbor. And certainly, knowing of one in Mrs. Pino's situation, common courtesy would have said to be of all the help you can. But, then, not everyone cares about common courtesy. There is still selfishness, and hatefulness, and sinfulness in the world.

For thousands of years our Father has been trying to get us—all of us—to treat each other like brothers. And for an equal number of years we have been refusing. "Do unto others as you would have them do unto you." Stupid! Silly! Out of date! Childish! Some people evidently think so. At least they don't think it applies to them. I wish those people could speak with Freddie, or Ruben, or Richard. Unfortunately, they cannot. They will have to speak with Mrs. Pino. You see, Freddie, Ruben, and Richard are all dead. They drowned.

"Do unto others . . ." Think about it the next time your brother is in need. And if you fail to act on it, for your own sake ask for forgiveness.

A Pebble On:
THE PACK IS STACKED AGAINST LITTLE JOHNNY

Proverbs 22:6a—"Train up a child in the way he should go . . ."

I saw a tragedy last Sunday morning. I hope I see it again next Sunday morning. For I would rather see the tragedy I saw than a greater one I fear will eventually occur.

I will call him Johnny. That's not his name, but for our purpose that's what I will call him. Johnny is in elementary school. He is in his formative years. And Johnny is the tragedy—or miracle as it may turn out to be.

You see, Johnny came to Sunday School and worship by himself last week. He's been doing it for some time now. Sometimes Johnny will ride with a neighbor to the church, sometimes when the weather is fair he will walk. Sometimes a member of his family will bring Johnny to the church and drop him off.

What's the tragedy I saw? Just that. Someone in Johnny's family bringing Johnny, dropping him off to go by himself. Johnny's father and mother have something else to do, more important. And so Johnny managed to get to the place that would give him some direction in life all by himself.

28

The story is repeated often in our society. However, I'm afraid it doesn't happen enough. For most Johnnys never manage to get to Sunday School and worship. They simply find more important things to do like the rest of the family.

How long little Johnny will continue to see to it that he gets himself to a place that can give him moral and spiritual instruction and guidance I don't know. I hope he will find strength in himself to continue the habit. But I'm afraid that one day Johnny will find it easier to sleep. Or one Sunday the family will make some plans that will require Johnny to be away, and that will be followed by another Sunday with some more plans, and another, and another.

I guess what I'm really saying is that the pack is stacked against Johnny. The chances of his continuing his present habits are small. The odds against him are too heavy. Johnny will find, further down the road, that his visits to the House of God will have to cease. The family has others things to do, more important.

Johnny isn't a poor boy. His family is one of means. They have what most families long for—two cars, a fine home, modern conveniences, the works. Now they are not millionaires, but they are well over the poverty line, materially.

And that's the tragedy. Johnny's family gives him everything he needs, except what he needs the most. And I guess, if you asked them, Johnny's family would say they love him. Certainly there would be an emptiness in their home should Johnny suddenly die.

But like I said, Johnny's chances are slim. There's

just too much going against him. There's always that slight hope for a miracle, however. So I guess we can hope. But in a few years if Johnny doesn't make it and he turns out wrong, don't be to hard on him. For as a youngster, he really tried.

Johnny isn't kin to you, is he?

A Pebble On:
IT'S WHERE YOU ARE

Proverbs 16:20—"He who gives heed to the word will prosper, and happy is he who trusts in the Lord."

Some time ago I read in the papers an account of a man in Phoenix, Arizona, who had rented an apartment but couldn't move into it because he had lost it! Actually, he couldn't find it. It seems that Charles Rowland had sold his photo-finishing business in Appleton, Wisconsin, and moved to Phoenix. Upon his arrival in Phoenix Rowland checked into a hotel. That same day he found an apartment and paid one month's rent in advance. However, he drove away without noting the address.

After 14 hours of driving around the city to locate the apartment, he notified a local newspaper of his plight. The fellow who had rented the apartment to Rowland read the article and called him at the hotel. It seems that the apartment was just two blocks, a couple of minutes, away from the hotel!

Then there was the case of Dr. Ellis Shenken, an ophthalmologist in Toronto, Ontario, Canada. Dr. Shenken was punched in the eye and as a result he lost one of his contact lenses. Dr. Shenken, unable to find the lens, got fitted for another soon thereafter. But the eye in which Dr. Shenken got punched kept discharging and his new lens kept popping out. It should have. You see, the lens which Dr. Shenken searched for but couldn't find had been pushed into his eyelid, where it remained unnoticed!

While a student in school, I worked in a grocery store to help defray my expenses. As I was stocking the shelf one day a gentlemen kept walking up and down the aisle looking for some product. Finally, he stopped in the section where the product should be located. After looking for quite a while for the product, he asked me if I knew where the product could be found. Reaching to the spot where he had been looking for several minutes, I picked up the product and gave it to him. His comment? "If it had been a snake it would have bitten me."

It wasn't long after that till I began a search early one morning for my glasses. After searching for several minutes about the house and failing to find them, I began to accuse one of the children or my wife of misplacing them. Seeing I was about to lose what little temper I had, Lynda started searching with me. She came into the room where I was searching and started to speak, only to have a wide grin come across her face. "Go look in a mirror," she said. I took the hint and suddenly realized that I was wearing the glasses I had so desperately been hunting!

Isn't it rather funny sometimes how we can search high and low for something, and then end up finding it in a place where it should have been so simple to find? These four stories could be multiplied by countless individuals who have searched for something only to find it in a place so close by.

Now there is a truth here that could be applied to countless realms. But for the sake of simplicity, let's try just one. Happiness. It's right where you are, if you can find it.

A Pebble On:
NO HELP WANTED

Romans 12:3a—"For by the grace given to me I bid every one among you not to think of himself more highly than he ought to think, but to think with sober judgment . . ."

The young man walked into the service station. Seeing his friend who owned the station in the rear, he yelled out: "Hi, Sam. How's business?" From the back of the station came the reply: "As usual." Sitting down next to the phone, the young man yelled again: "Mind if I use your phone?" "No, go ahead and help yourself," came the reply.

The young man picked up the phone directory, thumbed through its pages until he came to the correct page. Placing the directory next to the phone, he dialed the number. About that time the owner of the station walked up and sat down next to the young man. "How are you doing with that new boat and motor, Bob?" asked the owner. "Folks been telling me that they are seeing a lot of Bob Smith out at the lake hauling in the big 'uns. Sure sounds like you are getting your money's worth out of it," Sam continued.

Bob's party on the other end of the line had answered by that time and he held up his hand motioning for Sam to be quiet. As Bob started talking, Sam noticed that he was disguising his voice to keep from being recognized. Wondering what it was all about, Sam listened closely to the conversation.

"Is this Woodruff's Store?" asked Bob in the disguised voice. From the other end came the reply, "Yes, it is." "Could I speak to Mr. Woodruff," Bob asked in the muffled tone. "This is Mr. Woodruff speaking," said the party on the other end. "Mr. Woodruff, I was wondering about a possible job with you. Several months ago I saw an ad of yours in the paper where you said you needed someone to work there in your store as a salesman. I have some experience as a salesman and believe I could do you a top notch job," said Bob as he continued to use the fake voice.

"I'm sorry," Mr. Woodruff replied, "but that job has been filled for about six months now. Fellow by the name of Bob Smith contacted us and we hired him right away." "Is that right?" Bob continued. "Sure hate that. Would have loved to have worked for you. Maybe this Bob Smith fellow isn't doing too well and you could let him go and let me have that position?" Bob asked while Sam stared at him with puzzlement. "No, I'm afraid I couldn't do that," Mr. Woodruff replied. "Bob Smith is doing us a real fine job. Fact about the business is that he is one of the best salesmen we have ever employed." "Well, I appreciate talking to you Mr. Woodruff and I may call you again in the future," Bob said as he hung up the phone.

Sam couldn't wait to ask the question. "What in the world were you doing? I thought you had been working down at Woodruff's for about six months now," said

Sam. "I have," replied Bob. "Then why did you call about a job and talk in an unnatural voice?" asked Sam. "Well, Sam," said Bob, "you might say I was just checking up on myself."

I guess that's something we all need to do pretty often.

A Pebble On:
THE BEST ANSWER TO CRITICS

Luke 6:27—"But I say to you that hear, Love your enemies, do good to those who hate you."

Edwin M. Stanton lived from 1814 to 1869. He was a nervous, asthmatic, cranky, and contradictory lawyer who worked his way up after dropping out of college because of a lack of funds. Stanton served as the Attorney General in the Cabinet of President James Buchanan.

Stanton was also a sharp critic of Abraham Lincoln, and had many unkind words for the man who followed Buchanan as the President of the United States. He often spoke of Lincoln as "a low cunning clown" and even nicknamed him "the original gorilla." Stanton went so far as to suggest to a famous hunter of the time that he was a fool to wander over Africa trying to catch a gorilla when he could have easily found one in Springfield, Illinois.

After Lincoln was elected President, he was influential in acquiring a post as legal adviser to Simon Cameron, Secretary of War, for Stanton. Even after this favor, Stanton continued his harsh criticism of Lincoln.

Many people were shocked when Lincoln appointed

Stanton as the Secretary of War following the resignation of Cameron. It was hard for them to understand why Lincoln would give such a high, important post a to a man who had continually criticized him and his policy.

While Stanton was treating Lincoln in such a manner, Lincoln continued to show Stanton every courtesy. He never spoke to him harshly, or returned hateful remarks with hateful remarks. Lincoln appointed Stanton to the job of Secretary of War for one simple reason—Stanton was the best man for the job. Lincoln knew this, and did not let the ugliness of Stanton stop him from making the appointment.

On the night of April 14, 1865, Lincoln was watching a play entitled "Our American Cousin" from a box at Ford's theatre in Washington. During the play a man named John Wilkes Booth entered the box where Lincoln was sitting and shot the President in the head. During the confusion that followed Lincoln was carried to a little room where an attempt was made to save his life.

Into that room that night came several people. They watched—stunned—as their President lay dying. Among those who were there was Edwin Stanton, the man who had been so harsh and critical of the President, despite the fact that the President had shown him every courtesy and kindness. Looking down at the rugged form of a gentle man, Stanton spoke through the tears: "There lies the greatest ruler of men the world has ever seen."

A Galilean Carpenter once said: "Love your enemies and pray for your persecutors and those who treat you spitefully." Stanton had learned the hard way that this was the highest and noblest way of living ever given mankind. His criticism was finally silenced—by love.

A Pebble On:
BEING A PRUDE

II Corinthians 8:21—". . . for we aim at what is honorable not only in the Lord's sight but also in the sight of men."

I'm a prude. I will admit it. I'm a prude. And I use the word not in the sense of its meaning in the dictionary, but in the method which it has found itself used in today's slang language. In that language, you know, a prude is someone old-fashioned, less than a modern he-man. But, like I said, I'm a prude.

I'm a prude because I still believe in honesty. I don't believe in cheating or lying to my fellow man. When I charge a bill, tell a man I will pay that bill, I believe I should pay it. It may, under trying circumstances, be in small installments but if I live long enough, I will get it paid. I have given him my word and he has accepted it as the truth. He has put his trust in me and I cannot let him down.

I'm a prude because I still believe in kindness. I still think you should be kind to your fellowman instead of hard and harsh and rough. A kind word, a small gesture of kindness, a little gift can build lasting friendships.

I'm a prude because I believe in helping. I realize it is impossible for me to help everyone in the world and I'm not responsible for the whole world. I'm only responsible for the little corner I live in. I realize my inability to be all things to all men, but I do believe I can be something to some men.

I'm a prude because I believe in decency. I can see nothing good coming from speech that is dirty and filled with profanity. Some of the words, and their implications, in some of the songs on today's market turn my stomach. Some of the trash which passes for "art" on the screen of today would make Sodom and Gomorrah look like a fairyland.

I'm a prude because I don't drink. They tell us that 65% indulge in it now. Maybe that's what they want us to believe, maybe that is the correct figure. It doesn't bother me if 99 and 44/100% do it, to me it is wrong. And I hate the whole stinking mess when I pick up my paper and see the number of innocent people who suffer and die because of drink. We scream when a few innocent people die in war, and will not speak a word when thousands die because of drink on our highways.

I'm a prude because I believe in America. Despite all of it's faults, it is, to me, still the greatest country this world has ever known. I believe I owe my country more than my country owes me. I believe I don't have the right to criticize it unless I also try to make it better.

I'm a prude because I still believe in God. And to make me more of a prude, I still believe in a good God. I believe He is like a Father, and that He loves us, wants the best for us, and hurts when we shun Him and His way. I believe we will never achieve what we long for the most apart from Him.

41

I told you before I began that I was a prude. Now you know why. But you know what? I'm a prude with pride!

A Pebble On:
WHEN YOU ARE WILLING TO LOSE . . .

Luke 9:24—"For whoever would save his life will lose it; and whoever loses his life for my sake, he will save it."

James O. White, 44, thought his civilian job at McClellan Air Force Base was a waste of time and money. Doing the opposite of what most folks would have done, Mr. White took pencil and paper in hand and began to write a suggestion for the Suggestion Box.

He told the U.S. Government that the abolishment of his position as an Inventory Management Specialist was in the best interest of all concerned. Now that's something the average fellow wouldn't do! The average fellow would try to hang on as long as possible. But, then, Mr. White wasn't an average fellow.

The suggestion bounced through bureaucratic channels for several months until it finally reached the Air Force Logistics Command at Wright-Patterson Air Force Base in Dayton, Ohio. And along the way it no doubt caused many an eyebrow to be raised, and perhaps caused many a chuckle to boot.

At Wright-Patterson someone appreciated his idea— and agreed with him. So, in a short time, White's job was scrapped. There was no longer an opening for an Inventory Management Specialist.

There is an old law which says that one has to lose himself to find himself. Mr. White's actions were an example of that law being put into practice. He considered the job an unnecessary burden on the taxpayers. He saw a better way of getting the job done. And he was willing to risk his source of livelihood for the betterment of his employer. He had gotten self out of the way—and put a desire to do what was best above himself.

All of us could benefit from such an example. For many of us have never lost ourselves. We think of ourselves as the number one player in this game of life—and our thoughts hardly ever go beyond ourselves. We would seldom think there would be a better way of doing what we are doing, and certainly would not suggest it if there were—we might lose what we are doing!

One day years ago now a Carpenter told some friends of His that if they would lose themselves they could find themselves. In fact, He said, one could never find his true self until he had lost himself. And He went on to say that the person who was continually looking out for old number one would inevitably lose what he did have. The principle is true not only in religion, but the whole of life. When you are willing to lose then you are ready to find.

And I guess many of us are concerned about James O. White. We nearly always worry over those who lose themselves in service to others. But we shouldn't. It's true White lost his job as Inventory Management Specialist. But he got a check for $1,000 for his suggestion and was promoted to Supervisor. He lost himself to find himself—and a better job.

Truth is truth, in whatever area you find it.

A Pebble On:
A FATHER'S LOVE

John 3:16—"For God so loved the world that he gave his only Son, that whoever believes in him should not perish but have eternal life."

Alexander Ducat, 67, offered his life in exchange for the freedom of his son. Ducat, from Maryland, told authorities that he was willing to teach in North Vietnam in exchange for the release of his war prisoner son.

Ducat smiled despite the fact that tears were in his eyes when he told reporters of his offer. He said he offered to organize technical and vocational schools in Hanoi if the North Vietnamese government would free his son Bruce, age 29.

"I have completed a satisfying career and my life is approaching its twilight," Ducat, a former vocational educator, said. "Bruce has been a prisoner for four years. He has not seen his small daughter since she was an infant. The greatest happiness I could have, in the declining years of my life, would be to see him reunited with his wife and child."

This is not the first story of a father making a supreme sacrifice for his children. Many have been the parents who gave their life that their children might live, even as Mr. Ducat was willing to give his life for his son.

Beyond a shadow of doubt the greatest sacrifice was made some two thousand years ago. A Father found His children enslaved, hopelessly enslaved. He thought of some way to give them freedom. Then He saw that the only way to set His children free was for Him to give Himself as ransom for their freedom. And this He did.

You see, His children were captives of sin. And in order to free them from their sinfulness, the Father came down in the form of a Son. He dwelt with those living in sin, and He loved them so much and wished that they could be free from their sin so much, that He gave His life as a ransom for their freedom from sin.

The children did not deserve the gift from the Father. They had not earned it, in fact they actually had done many things to keep them from ever acquiring it. But while the children were unworthy of the Father's gift—while they were yet sinners—He died for them because He loved them.

And now the children of the Father can have freedom —real freedom—by simply accepting the Father's gift! But because freedom brings responsibilities, many of the children have elected to remain imprisoned. So despite the life-giving gift of the Father, many of His children are still not free because they refuse the gift. You see, the Father will not force His children to accept His gift of freedom. He will offer, but not force.

Mr. Ducat loved his son, more than he loved his own life. Mr. Ducat also knew what freedom is, and for that reason he was willing to give up his life for his son's freedom.

Maybe one day Bruce Ducat will come home to be with his wife and child. And perhaps one day those of us who are children of the Father will accept the Father's gift—and be free indeed!

A Pebble On:
TO LOVE IS TO SHARE

Hebrews 13:16a—"Do not neglect to do good and to share what you have ..."

One day three-year-old Amanda Smith got to visit a local fair in London. She had a really great time. She enjoyed herself so much. The only thing she regretted was that her baby brother, Georgie, wasn't with her at the fair.

After thinking it over for some time, and remembering how much the fair meant to her, she decided she wanted Georgie to go. So she took Georgie and set out for the fair. Several hours later the two were found a half-mile away—cold and hungry but unhurt.

It's a tender story if you will but think about it. A little child found something she liked. She found something worth sharing. And she wanted to share it with her little brother. Because she loved him, she wanted Georgie to have a chance at something which had meant so much to her. And she was determined to make sure that he had a chance to do exactly that.

Followers of the Nazarene are like little three-year-old Amanda. They have found something that means so much to them that they want to share it with those they love. And in order to share it with others, they are willing to sacrifice. Of course they learned this desire from the One Who gave it to them. He was so excited about the Good News that He had to share it with those around Him. Even when faced with danger and threat of life, He did not cease from sharing what great things He had found with those near Him.

Suppose for a moment that a doctor, having searched for many years for a cure for cancer, suddenly found that cure. Don't you think he would be so excited that he would want to share that discovery with everyone in the world? And especially with those who have cancer. Think of how much joy and happiness and pleasure it would give that doctor to see cancer patients cured of their illness because of the cure he had found.

That, too, is the feeling of those who have discovered the healing power of the Carpenter of Galilee. They have found a cure for the cancer of sin—selfishness, and prejudice, and hatred, and littleness, and all the other things that keep men from living the abundant life. The Followers of the Way have found something which gives their life meaning, and purpose, and hope. Why shouldn't they want to share it with those who are still searching?

Amanda found something that meant so much to her that she wanted to share it with a loved one—Georgie. And any doctor who discovers a cure for cancer and doesn't share it with the world would be a fool. It's just natural then that those who have found the Way wish to share with others.

To share our best with another is one of life's greatest privileges.

A Pebble On:
FOLLOW THE LEADER

Matthew 15:14b—"And if a blind man leads a blind man, both will fall into a pit."

In Kuala Lumpur, Malaysia, a cross-country race was held. The race was to cover a seven-mile course. Two hours after the race had begun, ample time for the runners to cover the course, none of the runners had returned. The officials, fearing that something might have happened, set out in automobiles to find the runners.

The officials found all of the runners six miles away, and sprinting in the wrong direction. Many of the runners had already covered distances of ten miles. A. J. Rogers, the association secretary, said the mixup apparently occurred when the lead runner took a wrong turn at the fifth check point and the rest followed him!

Sometimes this happens. We play follow the leader without knowing where the leader is going. We do things simply because someone else does them. We make our decisions because someone else has made the same decision before us. And while this is not always bad, it most certainly isn't always good.

All of us should be aware of where it is that we are

going. One of the greatest mistakes of so many in our society is that they are running as fast as they can, following the man in front of them, trying desperately to catch up, and not knowing where the fellow they are following is headed.

Occasionally someone will come along who will consider where it is that he wants to go. He stops long enough to study where following the man in front will lead. These people make up their own minds about which way the race should be going.

The Galilean was a Fellow like this. There was a full-fledged race going when He came upon the scene. All the runners were following the leaders. They were pushing with all they had to keep up, to be abreast, racing with the crowd. The leaders had always run their path, and they never questioned its authenticity. They simply took for granted that the runner in front was going the right way.

Then He came into the race. He saw where those who were supposed to be leading the race were headed, and He knew that that was not the path that the Judge had set for the race. So He stopped, took note of the roads, and headed off in another direction. Since he was the Leader in this new direction, the leaders that were going in the other direction became very angry that He should do such a thing. Why didn't He follow them like all the other runners? Of course, the only thing to do was to belittle Him, and eventually get rid of Him. He could prove dangerous to the course they were leading!

Somehow, this same idea of following the leader that

prevailed back then is still around today. If the first car passes an injured man on the highway, all the others are supposed to do the same. If one man takes a joke at Christian values, all other men who follow do the same. If one man shuns another man of different color, then we all must shun him. It's a game we play. We call it follow the leader.

I believe I would rather know where I'm going than to be in a hurry to follow the man in front of me.

A Pebble On:
WHEN TOMORROW COMES

Romans 14:10b—"For we shall all stand before the judgment seat of God."

Four-year-old Alison Hann complained to her parents one day that her stomach hurt. Her parents, Mr. and Mrs. Terry Hann of Hornchurch, England, took Alison to a doctor for examination. The doctor came back from making an X-ray of Alison's stomach and explained to Mr. and Mrs. Hann why her stomach hurt. The doctor told the girl's parents that she had swallowed 28 beads, a dog's bone, three plastic toy bricks, a deflated ballon, a toy dog, eight coins, some bird seed, sand, and leaves. You know, I would imagine that if you had all that in your stomach that you would have stomach pains also!

Now the story about little Alison Hann might startle us, or we might even find a touch of humor in it. But there is a higher truth which the incident brings to mind.

We are created, you see, in a certain way. The organs of our bodies are made to perform certain duties. Put food in our stomach and we get energy to perform our work, run our brain, and build our body. But fill that same stomach with junk—beads, bones, toy bricks, deflated balloons, toy dogs, coins, bird seed, sand, and leaves—and you will come up with a tummy ache.

Can we move now to another step, just a little higher? Man has about his makeup another part—we call it his spirit. Nurture that spirit with love and devotion and dedication and it will grow and give us the energy to perform countless good deeds for ourselves, our fellow-man, and our Creator. But fill that spiritual side of us with junk—booze, filthy reading, selfish greed, prejudice, indifference, hatred, jealously—and you will come up with a spirit that has a spiritual tummy ache.

No man with average intelligence would dare feed a child of his, or even himself, such objects as beads, bones, toy bricks, coins, balloons, and the like. Yet the same man willingly offers his soul only a diet of filthy reading, profane speech, indifference, and all the other junk which will kill the soul. And the diet he offers to his children is no better.

Our lives can get so cluttered up with things that have no lasting significance that we lose sight of those things which are most important. Eternity. Few people think seriously of it anymore. The only thing important is the here and now. "Don't come around me with this Carpenter bit, preacher. I have a house, good car, good job, money in the bank, booze in the cooler, and bets on the horses. Don't bug me, preacher, I have everything I need."

Maybe you do have everything you need. Maybe you do not. I will not argue the point. But how about tomorrow? When it comes, and it comes once to everybody, will you have everything you need?

Eternity may seem like along way off. But somehow it manages to get around to us. To all of us.

A Pebble On:
MORALITY VS. ECONOMICS

I Timothy 6:10—"For the love of money is the root of all evils; it is through this craving that some have wandered away from the faith and pierced their hearts with many pangs."

Don't give up on people! There's still goodness left is some of them! Mrs. Jean Cardon of Los Angeles is proof of that.

Mrs. Cardon was walking down a Los Angeles sidewalk one day when she found $100 on the street. She carried it to the police station and turned it over to the authorities.

"So, what's so great about that?" you ask. Well, I would agree that there would be several who would do likewise. But Mrs. Cardon was something of a special case in my book. Why? Well, for the simple reason that at the time she found the money she didn't have enough money for a bus ticket to the police station ten blocks away. In fact, she was flat broke. So she walked the ten blocks to the station to turn the money in. And to top it all off, she didn't even have a job!

Why did she do it? "I just followed my impulse," she said. Her "impulse" told her it was the right thing to do. She went on to add another comment. "Some people tell me I was foolish." Well, you could have predicted that. There are always some who call honesty foolish. To them it would be a simple case of "finders keepers, losers weepers."

Since turning in the money Mrs. Cardon has opened her first savings account in twenty years with a deposit of $700. No, she didn't get a reward for turning the money in. It seems that people heard of her deed and wanted to help a person with such high morals.

There is, within each of us, that "Impulse" which Mrs. Cardon spoke of. It's there, unless, of course, we have killed it with neglect. It is there to help us make the right decision. Did you notice that Mrs. Cardon said that her impulse told her it was the "right" thing to do? That's one reason that "Impulse" is there, to help us determine right from wrong.

For Mrs. Cardon it was a moral decision, not an economic one, which was called for. Money was involved here, but it was no basis for a decision. The only basis for a decision was what was right. Do you think that perhaps business could take a tip here? For many times there is a moral decision which over-rides an economic one. And maybe even for you and I there is a hint of help here. To spend our money like we should—with an obligation to do right. If we could follow the example, maybe we could change the fact that we spend twice as much on liquor as on the Carpenter's work.

Admittedly, money—too much or too little of it (for no one ever has just the right amount) —creates all kinds of problems for most of us. And we are often tempted to stretch our morals a little to catch up with our economics. But is it the money itself that creates the problem?

And if you should decide to take the tip and make the change with regards to money and economics, remember Mrs. Cardon's other remark. Some people will call you foolish.

A Pebble On:
JOHNNY SPENCE GOT WISE

II Timothy 3:5—". . . holding the form of religion but denying the power of it. Avoid such people."

There was a boy in South Carolina by the name of Johnny Spence. When he was 13 years of age he became a 7th-grade dropout. Like most other dropouts, Johnny found it tough sailing. While he didn't have many talents, he did have one. He had a talent for golf, and he used it.

When he was 17 he was the pro at a country club. Everybody liked Johnny. And for a 17-year-old, Johnny made good money. Johnny was a faithful church member, and this meant that on Sunday he didn't show up for work till after church. One Sunday the president of the club was waiting for him when he came to work. With the president was the governor of South Carolina, the mayor of the town, and other people on the VIP list.

When asked where he had been, Johnny said he had been to Church School and Worship. His superior remarked to Johnny something like this: "Well, you will have to quit that or we will find ourselves another pro. Being a church member is alright. I'm one myself. But don't let it interfere with business." So Johnny quit letting the Church interfere with his business.

Johnny soon became a golf instructor for some college coeds. Johnny fell in love with one of the girls. They began to go to parties where drinks were served. Johnny's sweetheart began to criticize him because he refused to drink with the others. So, to satisfy his sweetheart, Johnny began to drink at the parties.

Things went real well for the 7th-grade dropout. It wasn't long till Johnny Spence was making up to $5,000 some weeks. He also became not only a heavy drinker, but went the whole route—morphine, dope, you name it, he tried it.

Once his wife and mother poured his whisky down the drain. Johnny grabbed the shotgun and would have shot them, he said, had not an officer hit him on the head from behind. Soon they carried Johnny to a veterans' hospital for help. When Johnny tried to end it all by slashing his wrist and commit suicide, a guard overpowered him.

While Johnny was in the hospital, a chaplain came to see him. The chaplain told Johnny that the Galilean still loved him, wanted to help him, would forgive all he had done. Some men from the country club where Johnny had worked who were followers of the Carpenter came to visit him, pray with him, express concern for him. Soon Johnny was going to their meetings. Before long he was once again a follower of the Man of Galilee and a person with a new lease on life.

Johnny Spence tells his story wherever people will listen to him. Many groups want him to speak about his recovery. But some of those who want him to tell of his recovery don't want him to mention the name of the Galilean in his story. They think it is out of place to mention Him outside a church building. Funny thing about it is that it was the same type of people that helped get Johnny in the mess to start with. The only thing different now is that Johnny Spence is wise, he doesn't listen to these people anymore.

Maybe one day we will all get wise.

A Pebble On:
THE SPIRIT OF THE LAW

Ephesians 5:25b—". . . Christ loved the church and gave himself up for her."

There seems to be a vast swing toward the letter of the law and away from the spirit of the law in our society. People are more intent toward making sure that the law has been met legally than they are if the law has been met morally. I guess the deciding factor is that if one meets the law legally then he cannot be punished, while failing to meet the law morally doesn't bring court action.

A pretty good illustration of this happened in Memphis, Tennessee, some time ago. Willie T. Burton left home one morning to see an old, dirty, well-worn 1958 Dodge car parked in front of his house. When he returned home from work late that evening he noticed that the car was still setting there. Because it was nearly blocking his driveway, Mr. Burton called police. The police told Mr. Burton that, according to law, it was not setting near enough his driveway for them to ticket it.

Mr. Burton then asked the police to move the car because he was afraid that one of his two children might dart from behind the car and be struck by another automobile. He was told by police that, according to law, the had to set there five days before it could be towed away. Mr. Burton was certain that the car had been abandoned, but could not get it moved because of legal technicalities. The law set up to deal with the problem made the problem impossible to deal with.

There are several things like that in our world. Take the Church, for instance. It's very easy to become a member of most local churches. But because of technicalities set up to protect one's relationship with the church, it is nearly impossible to keep an honest membership roll of the church.

Most rules concerning membership in the church are set up to protect the membership, and to make it meaningful. However, we have completely forgotten the spirit of those rules and have taken them legally. So if a person's name is on the church roll, he is legally a member of the church even if he hasn't been in twenty years or given a dime during that time. The spirit of the rule—that the member be an asset to the church and to himself—is never taken into consideration. Only the legality of the rule. And, legally, they are still members. But morally, and spiritually, they are not.

You know, this type of dealing with things has a very deadening effect on people. It can destroy the very thing we set out to protect. If you don't believe it, ask Willie Burton. The car sat in front of his house for five days like the law said. But on the third day, Lisa Gail Burton, age 4, darted out from the car and was struck by another automobile. She was pronounced dead at the hospital.

More important than the letter of the law is the spirit of the law. And the method in which we approach it is often a matter of life and death—spiritually as well as physically.

A Pebble On:
THE GUILTY GO FREE

Matthew 12:34—"You brood of vipers! How can you speak good, when you are evil? For out of the abundance of the heart the mouth speaks."

You see it occasionally. It makes you sick at your stomach. It makes you hurt down deep inside where the pain cuts. It makes you wonder about what we call civilization, and justice, and even sometimes humanity itself.

I saw it the other day. It was in the paper. You probably saw it also. It wasn't headline news, but it might have served a good purpose if it had been. It read something like this: "Sensation hungry spectators, disappointed when a 19-year-old gas station attendant abandoned a suicide attempt, taunted him into jumping to his death from a 104-foot water tower Thursday.

"A fire department official said the youth, Juergen Peters, climbed an iron ladder to the top of the tower and threatened to commit suicide following a dispute at the filling station where he worked. He changed his mind and was climbing back down when the taunts began.

" 'Jump, you coward, jump!' someone shouted from the crowd. As Peters moved lower the taunts became louder. He hesitated, looked at the crowd, then began to climb back to the top. At the top he moved out on a parapet and flung himself off."

I'm sure the crowd went home with a sense of satisfaction, real fulfillment. They could feel something that the Romans used to feel when the Christians were thrown to the lions. The sight of twisted, crushed, broken, bloody humanity must be a very enjoyable sight to such people.

We speak a lot about our living in a civilized world. We brag on our scientific advances and revel in our mechanical accomplishments. We have learned more in the past ten years than man had learned in all of recorded history up to that time. And yet, with all our marvelous wonders, we sometimes are not anything more than blood thirsty animals.

We have counted the Church, and its Christ, out in our world. There's no place for Him, not in our modern world. He was a good crutch for the ignorant ages gone by, but the myth of Him just doesn't have any place in our world today. Few, indeed, are those who really believe that He has anything to offer our age. Most people have just outgrown the need for Him.

Let us suppose—and I know it is purely speculation —but let us suppose that those people who stood on that sidewalk beneath young Juergen Peters were real Followers of The Way, had decided to live by His Will. Peters would be alive today if that were the case. Have we outgrown Him, or have we merely become more ignorant with all our learning?

Well, at least one thing is clear when you look at the incident. All murderers aren't arrested. Some can walk away, perhaps to taunt—and kill—again.

A Pebble On:
WHO OWES WHOM?

I Corinthians 11:12b—"And all things are from God."

I guess you saw it. It was in the papers across the country. Russell H. Tansie of Oakland, California, filed a suit against the Creator in the amount of $100,000. Tansie filed the suit on behalf of his legal secretary, Betty Penrose, who blamed God for a lightning bolt which struck and destroyed her home in Phoenix some nine years earlier. Tansie officially charged God with "careless and negligent" control of the weather.

Well, it was more of a publicity stunt than anything else. We humans sometimes become little balls of ego walking around and finding a way to get our names before the masses means a lot to us. So some will stoop to anything for the sake of fame.

But, you know, it sets one to thinking. Who will represent the Diety at the hearing? Should He lose, who will pay the amount? Will this open up other suits against Him? Well, there's a lot of questions which come into our mind concerning the situation. Most of them are of very little importance. I doubt very seriously if the Creator would appear at such a hearing in the expected manner. Judging from past experience, we might as well forget the whole thing. A fellow named Job wanted to argue his case with the Maker only to learn that it was a great mistake.

There is another side to the questions that pop into one's mind when he gets to looking at this thing of suits against the Creator, and that is will the Creator get a chance to file suit against us for messing up His property? It doesn't take one long to make his answer when that possibility opens up! We had better leave well enough alone! For it is quite evident who will come up on the short end of the deal.

Betty Penrose waited nine years to file her suit against the Creator. I wonder if we have ever paused to consider the patience that the Creator has with us. We have literally been making a mess of His property, destroying His creation, wasting His products for countless thousands of years. And yet He doesn't strike us dead to get what is due Him. That is a mystery, an eternal mystery! The patience of the One above us as He sees what we have done and are doing with the things which are His.

There is also the possibility that if we are to charge Him with the things which we consider bad, He might in return place a charge upon us for the things we call good. That makes one stop pretty quick, for it is quite evident again who will come up short. I don't think I have enough money to repay Him for a single day of sunshine, much less countless other gifts which He gives me.

It appears that when it cames to suing the Creator, we had better leave well enough alone. It opens up too many possibilities which could and would leave us flat broke and eternally in debt.

And since we have thought about it, I guess we are already that way. In debt, I mean.

A Pebble On:
ON BEING RICH

Luke 12:22—"For life is more than food, and the body more than clothing."

Somewhere I ran across the story of a man who visited a certain home. The home wasn't much to look at, kinda run down and lacking even a good coat of paint. Outside the home, in the yard, a little boy and his sister were playing. They were laughing, and running, and having a good time. The man surveyed the situation, summed up that the family wasn't very well off.

He asked the small boy some questions about the home and family. The little boy told him that his father had not been able to work lately because of illness, and that his mother had to care for the father. When asked about his patched clothes and his bare feet, the youngster explained that he had not had any new clothes since his daddy got sick. After a long period of conversation, the visiting gentleman found out that the little boy and his sister had not been to a movie, or to get a cone of ice cream, or any of the normal accepted childhood pleasures for several months. Wanting to say something to help the boy and his sister face the difficult situation, the man spoke. "It must be awful bad to be poor."

Quick as a flash the youngster answered back. "Mister, we ain't poor. We just ain't got no money."

How true! How eternally true! He was happy. He loved his sister. His parents loved him. He knew why his family was in the shape it was in financially, and he didn't complain. Money could not have bought what he had.

How very shallow our judgments go sometimes. How very mis-placed our values of riches. We think the only rich people are the people who have money. How miserable life would be if we had to face it on that basis—being poor if we had no money.

We've made a terrible mistake here. And we have passed it on to our children. That mistake is thinking a person has to have a bankroll in order to be rich. What a poor, pitiable basis from which to judge richness. No man is poor who has character, and purpose, whose life has been touched by the Galilean Carpenter, who has love of God and love of fellowman. Every man is poor who lacks those things regardless of his bank account. Whoever uplifts civilization, though he die penniless, is rich, and future generations will erect a living monument to him in deeds. A great bank account can never make a man rich and often hides real richness from him.

A man is rich or poor according to what he is, not according to what he has. We are important because we are God's children, not because of position, or power, or money. No man is rich who has a poor heart. One of the first great lessons of life is to learn the true estimate of values. How poor are those whose major goal is a growing bank account. A rich mind and a noble spirit will cast over the humblest person a radiance of beauty which most millionaires will never know.

Don't pity the person who is lacking money. Pity only the person who is lacking in character, and purpose, who rejects the Galilean, and the Father, and has no love for his fellowman. For they are the poor ones. But those who are the opposite are rich far beyond the expression and means of mortal money.

A Pebble On:
LIFE ISN'T EASY

Matthew 7:14—"For the gate is narrow and the way is hard, that leads to life, and those who find it are few."

One thing one learns about life rather early is that it isn't meant to be easy. From the moment the baby leaves the protection of the mother's security, it begins to cry. And from that moment on life never lets up on its demands on those who try to take it seriously.

There are two attitudes one can take toward life. One is the take care of myself, don't care too much about the other man, don't get too involved attitude. This is by far the most traveled road of life for the simple reason that it places no demands upon us that we don't want it to. We can do as we please, or not do as we please. We are content just to live our lives out, patting ourselves on the back, telling ourselves we are doing all that we should be doing.

There is another attitude toward life. That attitude says life is a sacred trust, given to us by the eternal Father, and that it should be used for the benefit of Him and our fellowman. This way of living is very demanding. Very few are there who are willing to strive toward this life. It places demands upon us that we don't want, causes us to strive toward what the masses call the impossible. This is often a very lonely way of living, since those who have common goals are few in number.

Often we are tempted to give up, to call it quits, to say with the carefree lot that it is an impossibility to live toward that high calling. We are tempted to lower our goals, tone down our plea, and think more about ourselves.

But then we ultimately come back to this—life isn't supposed to be easy. It is supposed to be a challenge. And the very moment we cease working toward that high calling, we begin to deteriorate into nothing but a self-satisfied, selfish human that joins the don't care crowd.

When we get to the place where we are ready to throw in the towel and call it quits, what we really need is to know that what we are doing has some significance and lasting value to it. For as long as a person can believe that what he is doing has God's stamp of approval on it, he can face any obstacle that stands before him. But once he quits believing in his high calling, he is doomed to a life of selfishness.

Sometimes the night gets dark, awful dark. And you begin to question whether or not you should forget that calling so high. For your job becomes hard, and you see very little chance of it getting any easier in the future. In times like that the only thing that will sustain one is the knowledge that what he is doing has God's approval, that his efforts will not be in vain, and that his God will gladly pour out His grace on those who need it.

Life is easy only when we are selfish. It is hard when we choose the high road. And while it gets to be awful dark sometimes on the high road, we need to remember that daylight always follows darkness.

A Pebble On:
AS LITTLE CHILDREN

Matthew 18:3—"Truly, I say to you, unless you turn and become like children, you will never enter the Kingdom of heaven."

The day had been one of those rough ones. You know what I mean, for all of us have them. It seems like everything had gone wrong from the moment that I had gotten up. I had been on edge most of the day, and had been in a mood that even I didn't like myself in.

Then, to add to the woes of the day, it seemed like my son had purposely been doing everything he shouldn't have been doing. I had been real grouchy with him, had taken very little time to understand him or help him. It just seemed like he was constantly in the way all that day.

Why is it we all have days like that? I'm not completely certain as to the why, but I have some ideas. One is that we get in too big a hurry. Perhaps this is the biggest fault of our jet-set day. We live in too big a rush. Sometimes we meet ourselves coming back. We think that our much doing and fast going means good living. And I think we are wrong about that. Often we need to "be still and know."

Then, another reason why we have days when everything goes wrong is because we don't take one thing at a time. We get a half-dozen things going—any one of which we should be doing by itself—and then they all come at us at one time. And we forget to take them one at a time. The result—tension.

Still another reason for days when everything seems to go wrong is that we forget the eternal presence of the gentle Galilean Carpenter. We try to tackle all our problems, face all our situations, do all our duties alone. And life just wasn't designed to be run that way. We are partners, not proprietors. And we need to remember that we are working with Him. How often we need to talk things over with our Silent Partner.

Well, the day came to a close as they all do. After the children had their baths, it was time for our family prayers. I must admit I wasn't in the mood to say my prayers, and had it not been from sheer habit and concern for the children I would not have knelt down beside the bed that night. For some reason, I can't recall now, the girls in the family didn't say their prayers with us that night. It was just the two of us. I let my son say his prayer first, and then I intended to say a quick one and call it quits. He began in the usual manner, thanking God for several things. And then it happened. His tone of voice changed. And in his final petition, with a voice so sincere that I thought he was going to cry, he said: "And, dear God, make me a better little boy. Amen." I was stunned, and shocked, and humbled, and ashamed. I had only one petition, and it came from the heart: "Dear God, make me a better father. Amen."

The Carpenter once said that those who enter His Kingdom would have to come as a small child. I understand a little better now what He meant by that.

A Pebble On:
PERSISTENCE

Hebrews 12:1b—"And let us run with perseverance the race that is set before us . . ."

There is a story told about a certain little boy who wanted a watch. Day in and day out he pestered his parents about getting him a watch. His parents put him off every way they could. Finally he drove his parents to the breaking point. His father told the youngster that he didn't want to hear another word about a watch from him.

Well, for the rest of that week the lad said nothing about a watch. He knew that to do so would certainly bring some uncomfort to his sitting down place. However, Sunday soon rolled around and the family was gathered together for a period of devotion. It was the custom in the family for each member to learn a new verse of scripture and to recite it each Sunday during devotions. Every other member of the family had said their scripture verse when it came time for the small lad to quote his. Looking up with a very solemn face, he quoted his verse perfectly. "What I say unto you I say unto all, watch." Well, I'm not certain if he got his watch or the other thing. But one thing I can say for him—he was persistent.

And that's a quality all of us could use—persistence. For one of our faults today is that we give up too soon, call it quits after a single setback, let failure break us instead of make us.

There is very little a person cannot do in this life if he sets out to do it—and stays with it. One reason we don't accomplish more is that we are quick quitters. We get a setback or two and then we say it can't be done. We give up. We quit trying. But history is full of things that couldn't be done. And that means it is also full of men who did them.

The world looks up in admiration to a man who has staying-power. He doesn't have to have great brains, or great riches, or vast opportunities. But if he believes in something, and has the persistence to stay with that belief regardless of the praise or scorn he receives, the world ultimately will look up to him.

One reason there aren't any more people with persistence than there are is the simple reason that it takes a big man to try again, or to stick out the ship when the waves get high. Anyone can quit. Anyone can get into a lifeboat and float to safety. But the man with persistence is hunting neither safety nor another mission. He has something he wants to do, and he believes he can do it. So he stays with it, come what may. Then one day he finally accomplishes the impossible.

Great and good goals aren't easy to accomplish. They require great and good men to accomplish them. And great and good men are men who keep on keeping on. I believe God wants a man who says, "I can." I believe God wants a man who will try again.

"All things are possible . . ." He is waiting to see if you believe Him. If you do, try again.

A Pebble On:
GETTING USED TO THE DARK

II Corinthians 2:11—"To keep Satan from gaining the advantage over us; for we are not ignorant of his designs."

I went to the movies the other day. First time in about a year that I had been. I'm not about to spend my hard earned two dollars to see filth and trash presented as though it was the ideal. But there was a Walt Disney production playing so I took the children and enjoyed the movie.

As I entered the theater, it was dark and I could hardly see. I moved slowly down the aisle, found a row where a seat was empty—I thought! But after sitting in someone else's lap for a split second, I fumbled on down the row till there was an empty seat. Talk about being dark, it was dark in that movie-house!

But you know, something happened to the darkness in that theater. After I had been in the darkness a short period, I began to get accustomed to it. Why, I could even make out which seats were empty! It wasn't long before that theater wasn't too dark at all. I could find my way around without a bit of trouble.

Something like this has happened in our society. The darkness seems so dark at first, but if you sit in it long enough, you get the impression that it is getting brighter. Time was when sin was called sin, when you could tell the good from the bad, but for many that time is slowly disappearing now. We have sat in the darkness until we have gotten use to it, even get the false impression that new light is breaking.

An alcoholic isn't a drunkard now. He has a new name, and the darkness has given him a new position. An alcoholic now is a sick man, not a sinful one. His alcoholism has no moral overtones about it. We use to call it sin, but now it is a disease. A disease which we manufacture, bottle, advertise, sell from an open counter, regulate (?) by the state, and collect taxes to build a better society on! Getting use to the darkness, aren't we?

Adultery now has a new name—free love! And it has several advocates, both in and out of the Church. It isn't sin anymore, it is situational ethics. And a movie star can have a baby out of wedlock one week and gain the admiration of millions on national television the next week! Getting use to the darkness, aren't we?

Murder will get you a hung jury, and sometimes three years in the pen at the most. And if you can provide the money to get the right lawyer, you still go scot free. We are a little more civilized than our forefathers. We believe in being lenient. The darkness is looking brighter now.

Strange, isn't it, that you can't get use to the darkness all at once. You have to sit in it awhile. And then it doesn't look dark anymore. Slowly, little by little, we get use to it.

But the Light of the world is still in the world, and men who love good and hate evil are still attracted to Him. And, strange as it may seem, men who love evil still hate the Light. For you see, when the Light comes they have no place to hide.

A Pebble On:
I'M A RICH MAN

II Corinthians 8:9—"For you know the grace of our Lord Jesus Christ, that though he was rich, yet for your sake he became poor, so that by his poverty you might become rich."

I'm a rich man.

Some people, I know, will deny that. Looking at my salary, my bank account, and what possessions I have that I have acquired with my money, they by no means consider me a rich man. They wouldn't even go as far as to say that I was in the "middle" bracket, much less the "upper" bracket. But, like I said, I'm a rich man.

I'm a rich man. I'm rich because of my heritage. I came from a home where parents loved me, provided for my needs to the best of their ability, sacrificed things they very much needed so I could have advantages they never had.

I'm a rich man. I have a wife who loves me. She puts up with all my faults, stands beside me, pulls for me when the going is rough. She is no Hollywood star, but most of the stars of Hollywood could not hold a light to her when it comes to real beauty.

I'm a rich man. I have three wonderful children. Three children who give hope and promise of a better tomorrow. I love them, want the best for them, and try to bring them up in a Christian home like my parents did before me.

I'm a rich man. I have a job. A very meaningful job. Not much money in it, nor prestige. But it gives me a chance to help my fellowman, to lift the sights of others to a higher level, to give my life to a Cause that will leave the world a better place in which to live. I will probably never "reach the top" of my profession, but I can face life knowing I did my best in the job which I felt my Creator wanted me to do. I have a job which I consider important because He considers it important.

I'm a rich man. I live in a free country. Millions and millions of people cannot know the richness of that. They live behind iron curtains, or under the shadow of a dictator. Millions more here in the country where I live have never realized that freedom is an obligation, not a license. Thus they are poor. Poor because they have not learned that freedom is not a license to drag men down into the depths of filth, but that freedom is an obligation to lift myself and my fellowman to greater and greater heights, pressing on toward that high mark to which our Maker calls us.

I'm a rich man. I have friends who are friends. They stay with me through the good times and the bad. They encourage me. They cause me to try harder. They keep me from giving up. When the clouds of darkness are around me, these friends of mine are beside me. They are true friends. The doors to their homes are open to me, as mine is to them.

I'm a rich man. I have found what many are still

searching for. I have found forgiveness, and understanding, and help. I found them in a crucified Galilean. He takes my weaknesses and makes me strong. He takes my fears and makes me brave. He takes my doubts and makes me believe. He assures me of what every man wants to know, that there will be life after death for me.

Like I said, I'm a rich man. Oh, by the way, could I borrow a dime?

A Pebble On:
"I DON'T UNDERSTAND"

Amos 5:24a—"But let justice roll down like waters . . ."

The little boy had just listened to an ad on the radio. With his questioning eyes gazing at his mother he spoke some penetrating words. "Mother," he said, "I don't understand." "You don't understand what, dear?" asked the mother.

"Well, the man on the radio said that if we sold more whiskey we could collect more taxes and help our schools. But the minister said in church recently that whiskey hurt and killed many people and that we should not drink it. I'm confused because I don't know who is right. If the taxes from whiskey go to our schools, shouldn't we try to get everybody to drink more whiskey so we can have more taxes? And if that is true isn't Mr. Smith, the alcoholic who lives down the street, the best fellow in town? After all, he buys more whiskey than anyone else and that means he pays more taxes into our schools than anyone else. Why do people treat him like a bum when he is doing more than anyone to help support our schools? Mother, why can't I buy whiskey and help support the schools?"

The little boy continued. "There's another thing I don't understand, Mother. You remember when they took that artificial sweetener off the market because they found that it had caused cancer in some mice? You remember they said that for it to cause cancer in a human that the human would have to use large amounts over a long period of time? But they immediately took it off the market. Yet on television that man keeps telling us that cigarettes cause cancer, but they don't take cigarettes off the market. Why, Mother?"

"And, Mother," the small child continued, "something else puzzles me. That man who you and daddy said was drinking when he ran into the other car and killed that little baby, why didn't he go to jail? They put the man in jail who had been drinking and shot his wife. Why didn't the man go who killed the baby? Is it worse to kill someone with a gun than it is with a car? Mother, are you deader from a bullet than from a car?"

"There's something else, too, Mother. That man who lost his month's pay check at the racing rack was really helping the state, wasn't he? I know he was because I read in the paper that betting was permitted so the state could collect taxes on it. Mother, does that man have lots of money? If he doesn't, why doesn't the state help pay his bills and feed his family? Looks like they would, for he was helping the state. He is such a good man to give the state his pay check when his family needed it so much."

"And there's another thing, Mother, that I don't understand. Who is the bad person, the man who leaves his keys in his car or the person who steals the car? I thought the car was the man's property and that he had the right to expect other people to leave it alone. But the ads on television said the man made the boy a crook by leaving his keys in his car. The ad didn't say the boy shouldn't steal the car. Mother, should we lock our doors when we leave home to keep a good boy from breaking in and going bad?"

"Mother," the boy continued, "There's one other thing I don't understand. When Uncle Joe died we went to the Church and the preacher made a speech. But Uncle Joe never did go to church while he was living. Why did we take him to the church when he died? If you go to church when you die, does that mean you will go to Heaven? Mother, could you explain to me? I don't understand."

The little boy didn't understand. But there is one thing that we do understand. He isn't by himself.

A Pebble On:
WHY DID HE COME?

Luke 4:43—"I must preach the good news of the Kingdom of God to the other cities also; for I was sent for this purpose."

I wish to dispute something you have heard all your life about the Galilean. And I want to do it in such a manner that you cannot possibly misunderstand me. I wish to make myself explicitly clear on the subject. I don't want you to think there is a misprint or that I don't mean what I say.

Now, with that as a foundation, brace yourself for the statement I'm about to make. The Galilean did not come to get us into Heaven. There, now, I have said it. And I mean exactly what I have said. He did not come to get us into Heaven.

I know what you have heard all your life. I know what you have been led to believe. I know what some well-intentioned fellow has spent much time trying to tell you. But I still want you to know that this much is true—He did not come to get us into Heaven.

I had heard that this was the reason He came, to get us into Heaven. I had heard that all the days of my life. Every fellow on the radio, every fellow in the church building, every fellow bringing me literature has been telling me that this was the reason He came—

to get us into Heaven.

In growing up I read it in some of the literature. Becoming an adult I continue to read it in some of the literature. Some fellows have made an extensive search and have even listed the things I have to do if I want to go there. Without these things, they say, I can never make it to Heaven. Despite what they have written, despite what they have said, I still want to make one thing clear—He did not come to get us into Heaven.

Now somebody is heading to get their Good Book and are about to take pencil in hand and write and straighten me out. I already get quite a bit of their literature in the mail. Now I am about to be deluged with it. It will come in bundles. Letters telling me what I have to do, what steps are necessary, what rules I have to follow to get there. They are already quoting from the Good Book some words that they are going to put down on paper and help me get straightened out on this matter. But it matters not if I get ten thousand letters, it will not change the truth. Nor will it keep me from making one thing crystal clear—He did not come to get us into Heaven.

Some of them are boiling now. Their faces are turning red. Their blood pressure is going way up. They are wishing they could stand in my face and quote it to me. Despite that, I wish to say once again that He did not come to get us into Heaven.

You see, there is one fact that we always overlook. That is that we cannot get into Heaven unless Heaven first gets into us. And that's the reason He came—to get Heaven into us!

A Pebble On:
HE'S THERE, TOO

Genesis 28:16b—"Surely the Lord is in this place; and I did not know it."

Sam put on his top-coat and picked up his briefcase and walked to the door. Saying good-by to the rest of the family, he proceeded to his car. He backed out of his driveway and headed down the road to the office. At the intersection he looked both ways and then started across. That's when it happened.

There was a terrible screech, tires grinding on the pavement coming to a sudden and complete stop. Sam jumped, looked toward his right to see a big tractor-trailer transport truck bearing down on him. In an instant his instinct told him to brace himself, to prepare for a terrible accident. The truck was about to crash into his small foreign made car. He braced and waited. But, miraculously, the driver of the giant truck managed to get the big rig stopped just prior to the anticipated collision.

With a sigh of relief and thankfulness, Sam uttered a quick prayer. Now it's only fair to say that Sam was not normally a very religious man, living mostly by his own creeds and just not having much time or interest in the kid stuff. But for some reason, he spontaneously let it slip. "Thank you, Lord," he said, suddenly remembering that there was Someone beyond

90

himself.

Sam and the driver of the truck got out and surveyed the situation. "Man," said the truck driver, "you are a mighty lucky person. Just a split-second difference in timing and you very probably wouldn't be around this old world right now. You had better be thankful that I had my brakes re-worked just last week. I would hate to think what would happened if I had not. And I started to put it off, but changed my mind at the last minute and went ahead. Buddy, you had better thank goodness that you are still alive."

"Mister," said Sam, "I have already thanked goodness." In a few moments Sam was on his way to the office again. At a service station along the route he took he saw Bill. Bill was a friend of his who worked in the same office. Bill was also the "religious" guy in their group—a regular church-goer. Sam wheeled in to speak to Bill and tell him about the truck.

"Say, Bill," hollered Sam out his window as he pulled alongside his religious friend, "the Lord is really taking care of me this morning. I pulled out in front of this big truck, but the Lord performed a miracle and stopped it just before it got to me. It sure is great how the Lord takes care of us, isn't it?"

"It sure is," said Bill. "He performed a miracle for me this morning, also." "He did?" Sam asked excitedly. "What happened? Did you like to get hit by a big truck also?" "Not quite," said Bill. "He just kept me from pulling out in front of any."

Strange how we can find Him in the "miracles" and not in the everyday events, isn't it?

A Pebble On:
THE GREATEST PART OF THE FAITH

**Mark 16:15—"And he said to them, "Go into all the world
and preach the gospel to the whole creation."**

I made what was, to me, a startling discovery recently.
I was reading about what happened on that Good Fri-
day in Jerusalem nearly a couple thousand years ago.
I read again how they hung that Man among men on
those two sticks of wood. I could feel the blows of the
hammer as they drove the nails into His palms. I could
feel the jar as the cross was dropped into its hole, and
came to rest with a terrific jolt. The flesh ripped, and
blood spurted.

You remember the rest of the events. You remember
how the crowd jeered at Him, made fun of Him, jok-
ingly dared Him to come down. It was a scene that has
been repeated often in the history of mankind. Over
and over again that lowly Galilean has been nailed to
those two pieces of wood. Many times we have stood
around jeering at Him, making fun of His claims, slashing His side with our selfish spears.

But you can remember, also, that the story didn't
end on that dark day. Finding an unused tomb in a
garden nearby, they laid Him in it. And then, because
the next day was an especially holy one, hardly anyone
moved. But Saturday is always followed by Sunday, and

on Sunday those who loved Him found what all who have loved Him since have found—an empty tomb.

I said I recently made what was to me a startling discovery. All my life I had thought of that cross and that empty tomb as the most dynamic events in history. I had always considered these as the top jewels to place on a crown of greatness. But now I see that they weren't the greatest part of His Faith. Now I can see that for all these years my sight just did not go far enough to find the most tremendous event in the history of mankind. Now I can see what the greatest part of this Carpenter's Faith is. And it is amazing!

He entrusted the work of His Church to those eleven men, those disciples, who had just prior to the resurrection betrayed Him! That, without a doubt, is the grandest thing about Him—that He trusted common people with the responsibility of His Church! Can you see that? Can you understand what it means? That He should give the greatest responsibility ever known to mankind to these eleven men is without question the highest sign of His love and trust in mankind.

He entrusted His Kingdom not to the high and mighty, to the great and gallant, to the brave and brilliant—but to common people! And He goes on entrusting His Church to common, plain, ordinary folk!

How great His trust in us! That He should give to plain folk the tremendous privilege of carrying on His Work speaks to His great trust in the common man! No one would have dared to trust those eleven men with such a great responsibility except that Nazarene.

No one else has such a trust in common folk like you and me.

Next time you are inclined to lose hope in mankind, give it a thought.

A Pebble On:
HIS IS A GREAT LOVE

Romans 5:8—"But God shows his love for us in that while we were yet sinners Christ died for us."

He endured the pain, the hurt, and the cruel remarks only because of His great love for us. Because of all our hatefulness, our stinginess, our sinfulness, He died upon that ugly cross. He loved us enough to take every sorry thing about us upon Himself and to pay for our unworthiness.

He wanted us to have the best and because of it He died for us. He wanted so much for us to love each other and because of it He died for us. He wanted a world free of war, and hatred, and every other ugly thing and because of it He died for us.

But we scorned Him. We took His love and made fun of it. We beat Him, laughed at His Way, took Him out and nailed Him to two pieces of wood. Then we stood around, drank our booze, gambled for His clothing, and mocked Him as He bled to death.

For nearly two thousand years now He has been trying to get us to understand that this is His world and that no way will work in His world but His Way. But we humans know more than He does. So we go on killing, robbing, and cheating, and lying, and making fun of Him and His Way.

It isn't popular to be a follower of His. You will still be made fun of, scorned, and laughed at. You can't get ahead in life by practicing His principles, so we are told, and we must all get ahead. We take followers of His and make them sissies in our movies. We show them as weak, insecure, unstable people. Most of the time we picture them as some sort of holier-than-thou hypocrite.

We have twisted His Way, perverted His teachings, misused His Church, wasted away His material goods. And our world is still searching for that something that is missing. Man is still the only animal on the face of the earth that will kill for revenge, and we call him the only civilized animal.

How great must be the hurt in His heart. To see what He had planned for us and what we have done with that plan. To see what great things He has prepared for us and then to see how we have scorned His Way. To have love that would allow His own Son to die for our sinfulness and then to see that love refused. How patient He is. Why He did not sweep us away centuries ago is beyond our understanding.

No, we can't understand it all. No one can. But we can understand one thing and that is that He loves us more than we can ever understand. We know He will accept us with all our ugliness and unworthiness. We know He will give us life and love. We know His power is greater than death, and apart from Him there is no life at all.

It seems that after two thousand years we humans would get around to trying His Way. But, like He said, we are ignorant. And I guess that's one reason He died for us.

A Pebble On:
THE GREAT DREAM

Joel 2:28—"And it shall come to pass afterward, that I will pour out my spirit on all flesh; your sons and your daughters shall prophesy, your old men shall dream dreams, and your young men shall see visions."

We used to be a nation of dreamers. Some of that is missing now, but we have it as part of our heritage. Our forefathers, those who founded our country, were dreamers. They dreamed of a country where man would be free, where he could live in dignity and hope and promise of a better tomorrow.

They lived that dream, believed in it so much they were willing to give their lives for it. Nothing could stop them from reaching out for that dream—not even all the combined power of the King of England. They took that dream and with it they beat the unbeatable foe, they conquered the unconquerable land, they traveled the untravelable roads. What great dreamers they were!

But they were not the greatest dreamers this world has had. There was a small group of men who had even greater dreams than did the founders of our country. Back nearly two thousand years ago there was a group of eleven men who had a dream—a great dream. They dreamed that they could conquer the world without ever lifting a sword or firing a gun. They dreamed that one day every man, woman, and child could and would share with them the new faith they had found. They dreamed that one day this world would be ruled by love.

It was a great dream they had—so great, in fact, that the world thought they were crazy. The world laughed at them, ridiculed them, even persecuted and killed them. But the dream could not be destroyed. It lived on. They planted that dream of a world ruled by love in the hearts and minds of other men. The dream lived and grew. Soon that dream had conquered men of all climates, all classes, all races.

There are those who are still dreaming that dream today. They are inspired by a Carpenter Who touched the hearts of common men as no other Man. He planted that dream in their hearts, nourished it, watched it grow. It is the dream of a world where men are brothers, where we help instead of hurt, share instead of steal, give instead of grab. It is a dream of a world ruled by brotherly love.

A foolish dream? An unrealistic dream? An illogical dream? Yes, it has been called all those things. But that doesn't stop men from dreaming it and from trying to make that dream come true. It is, in a way, an unfulfilled dream. But men still search after it.

The call goes out from this Galilean Carpenter today for more dreamers. Few there are who dare to give themselves to that dream. It seems unreachable to most people. It is certainly a big dream, and requires the best there is in a man. For this reason, very few dare dream that dream. For it is a challenge, the world's greatest challenge. It isn't a dream for sissies, or weaklings, or lazy men. No, it is a dream for men, great men.

If you are a dreamer looking for a dream to give yourself to, there is none greater in all the world. And one day, with His help, the dream will come true.

A Pebble On:
LIKE FATHER, LIKE SON

Matthew 5:48—"You, therefore, must be perfect, as your heavenly Father is perfect."

My study was located in a storage room (or what was supposed to be a storage room) directly behind our home. It was a very small room to begin with, and once you put my books and supplies and machines in it you could hardly turn around. It was really too small, but it was the best we could come up with at the moment and I had to bear with it until better days came along.

One day I was having one of those days when everything seemed to go wrong. It was a day when I wished, and most folks around me, that I had stayed in bed. My desk was covered over with matters that needed my attention, correspondence was lagging, and there were other matters pressing.

I was sitting in my study, half mad at myself and half mad at my lack of space. Then, without knocking, in came my son Timmy and proceeded to sit down behind me. I started to turn and tell him that there wasn't room for him in the study, but I waited for I knew that if I spoke at that moment I would be harsh with him. So I went about my work, listening as he began taking paper from the waste basket and books from the shelf. He nearly lit the fuse when he spoke. "Daddy," he said, "do you have a pen?" Well, I reached into my pocket and gave him my pen. I then tried to continue my work. But it seem that everytime I turned around I bumped into him. So, my temperature rising, I turned to scold him and send him back into the house. Upon turning, I was stopped cold by what I saw!

Timmy had laid out before him some old papers he had taken from the trash can, some of my books from the book shelf, and with pen in hand he was marking on a sheet of paper. He had made himself a make-shift desk that was in something of a mess. Now, most of the time when Timmy wants to know what I'm doing out in the study I tell him that "I'm studying." I looked at him there, he paused for a moment and looked up, and after thinking for a few seconds he began to write again. "What are you doing, son?" I asked him. He looked me in the eye as only a son can do and then gave me his answer with a little grin on his face. "I'm studying, Daddy."

I didn't say anything else to him. I turned back around and pretended to go back to work. But I didn't do much work for the next few minutes. I just sat there thinking how proud I was of my son. It made me feel just as big as a man can get to know that my son wanted to be like me, to do what I do.

But then a greater truth came to me. My Creator was telling me that this was really what He wanted from me. He wanted me to be like Him. I still think about that often. How good He must feel when we act like Him, do what He does, act like we were His sons. "Wouldn't it be a good world," I say to myself, "if we wanted to be like Him as much as Timmy wants to be like his father."

It sure would.

A Pebble On:
I'M TIRED OF THESE FOLKS

Matthew 7:15-16—"Beware of false prophets, who come to you in sheep's clothing but inwardly are ravenous wolves. You will know them by their fruits. Are grapes gathered from thorns, or figs from thistles?"

The following item recently appeared in the paper. "The author of the disparaging book, *The Passover Plot*, which states that Christ's crucifixion was faked to fulfill Old Testament prophecies about the Messiah, now questions the whole authority of the Christian church.

"Now Dr. Hugh Schonfield, in *Those Incredible Christians*, lashes out at what he calls 'vested beliefs and ecclesiastical rubbish.' The 68-year-old Jewish scholar is allegedly without a religious creed of his own, believing in God as 'pure spirit.' "

Well, now, how about that! He is a man who, he himself admits, doesn't know what he believes telling millions of other people that their belief is rubbish. Well, personally, I'm tired of folks like Dr. Schonfield. I'm tired of these self-appointed authorities who don't know what is right except that everybody else is wrong.

Yes, I'm tired. Tired of all the people who say God is dead who never knew He was alive. They live in their ivory palaces behind the sacred walls of education and spin out fancy theories about the nothingness of God. They never go down to the grave and watch a mother lay her child into the cold, hard earth. They never go to the hospital where the father of four young children is dying with cancer. They aren't ever called by the wife whose husband is an alcoholic. But they are sure, after reading the textbooks, that there is no God.

I'm tired. Tired of the people who say the Bible is a lie who never have even read it. Our society is full of them, these intellectual illiterates who speak in pure ignorance of the subject matter.

I'm tired. Tired of people who say the Church of today is irrelevant because we haven't been able to provide everybody with a mansion on the hill, a high income, a "meaningful" job, and the best social standing.

I'm tired. Yes, I'm tired of those fine people who say they can accept Christ as a great moral teacher but not as the Son of God or the Savior of men. Little do these people realize the absurity of their statement. A good moral teacher but not God? If He wasn't the Son of God, indeed God Himself, and did what He did, and said what He said, then He was a blundering, blind, ignorant fool. Stupid. Crazy. He was either Who He said He was, or He was a crazy idiot. But you will have to accept one description of Him. God incarnate or stupid madman. Unfortunately, the New Testament just doesn't leave room for you to classify Him as "a great moral teacher, but not God Himself."

Yes, I'm tired of these know-it-alls who don't know

what they believe. And let me add just one final word to them. They say they are searching for truth. If this be true, then maybe one day they will find what many of us have already found.

You see, we have already found Truth. We found it in a lowly Nazarene, apart from Whom no Truth can ever be found.

A Pebble On:
WHAT IS FREEDOM?

II Corinthians 3:17—"Now the Lord is the Spirit, and where the Spirit of the Lord is, there is freedom."

Freedom. Millions are in search of it. They want what our constitution guarantees them. Freedom of speech, freedom of expression, freedom of the press. And they are taking these rights of theirs, these freedoms, for they are tired of being enslaved by the society around them.

Have we ever thought through this word freedom? What do we mean by it? How does one give an explanation of freedom? Just what does it mean to be free? Our world is full of people now who have, they think, found the definition to the word. Tired of all the old restraints and restrictions, they are excercising their freedom. They fill the stands full of pornography and smut because they have the freedom of the press, a right guaranteed them by the constitution. They are on the warpath to get any mention of a Higher Power out of our official society because the freedom of religion guarantees them this right. And the list could go on and on, people who are exercising their rights to get away from the old restraints and restrictions, to gain freedom.

107

Nearly two thousand years ago a lowly Nazarene told a story about people like these modern-day searchers for freedom. This Nazarene said there was a young man who came to his father, demanded his share of the estate while he was young enough to enjoy it. The father gave in to his wish, for the boy had the right to the money. Soon the young man had packed his bags and headed for another country. He was tired of all the old restraints and restrictions of his society. He was tired of people telling him that he couldn't do what he had the right to do. What he wanted was freedom. And as he walked down that dusty road away from the father he felt this freedom in his soul. He was free at last, free to do as he pleased. There was no longer anyone to cram any religious doctrine down his throat. Finally, he found what he had searched for all his life—freedom!

But the Carpenter didn't end the story there. Many of you remember it. He said that before long the young man's money was gone, and with it went his freedom. He had to go to work, to give up his freedom in order to survive. The best job he could get was feeding the pigs. Finally, amid all the filth, the young man came to his senses. He got up and went home to seek his father's permission to work as one of the hired hands on the family farm. He was willing to take the lowest place in his old slavery rather than the highest position in his new freedom.

What is freedom? Well, never make the mistake of thinking that freedom is a matter of rights. It isn't. It is a matter of right. There is no freedom except spiritual freedom. And no man can become free until he has become a slave to something higher and greater than himself.

Freedom? Somehow I have an idea that those who are crying out the loudest for the freedom to do as they please will one day come to themselves. For the more they get of what they want, the less they will want of what they get.

"Make us captives, Lord, and then we shall be free."

A Pebble On:
WRITING A BOOK CHANGED HIS LIFE

Psalms 147:5a—"Great is our Lord, and abundant in power . . ."

Back in the second half of the 19th century there was a soldier by the name of Lew Wallace. He was a major general for the Union forces during the War Between the States. Lew Wallace was also a lawyer, and a states-man of some note. He served as governor of the New Mexico Territory from 1878 till 1881 and as minister to Turkey from 1881 till 1885.

Like many others, Lew Wallace found that as a grown man he had no religious beliefs. He often thought about this, especially when he was around some others who were strong in their belief. He even talked with Robert Ingersoll, the well-known atheist, for several hours once. Ingersoll tried to prove to Wallace that the Bible was an unworthy book.

Following a visit with some friends once, Wallace spent some time in deep thought about what the friends had discussed—God, Christ, the Bible, etc. Somehow Wallace had felt left out in the conversation. The reason was simple—he knew very little about the sub-jects.

Following that conversation Wallace made up his mind to write a book about what his friends had been talking about. The reason he decided to write a book was that he might make an in-depth study of the Bible. He knew that unless he had some primary reason to study the Bible that his study would be haphazard and would soon end.

So for the next several years Lew Wallace spent what time he could reading and studying the Bible. He read books related to the Bible, books that put light and understanding on the Bible. He also read books that shed light on the times during which certain events in the Bible took place.

For more than seven years Lew Wallace worked on his book. He developed his theme around the life of Christ. Since he knew hardly anything about the Nazarene, he made Christ the secondary figure in the story—kept Him in the background.

It was while he was serving as governor of the New Mexico Territory that Wallace put the finishing touches on the book. It wasn't a pleasant time to write for the governor, especially since his life had been threatened by none other than "Billy-The-Kid" himself!

Soon the book was finished. It was to become one of the most famous books ever written. Wallace named it BEN HUR. It was translated into several languages. In 1927 it was made into a motion picture. In 1959 it was re-shot, this time into one of the most spectacular motion pictures made up to that date. BEN HUR still enjoys good sales even today.

But the most important thing about this story is that Lew Wallace, the unbeliever, became Lew Wallace, the believer, because of the research on the book BEN HUR.

Many, indeed, are the paths the Nazarene uses to speak to us.